MATH STORIES

×	MULTIPLICATION
÷	DIVISION

JOYCE M. SCINTO

New Readers Press

ISBN 0-88336-747-5

Copyright © 1992
New Readers Press
Publishing Division of Laubach Literacy International
Box 131, Syracuse, New York 13210-0131

Printed in the United States of America

9 8 7 6 5 4

Table of Contents

LEVEL 1

Multiplying and dividing mostly one- and two-digit numbers. All problems, but not all steps, are set up.

LEVEL 2

Multiplying and dividing larger numbers. All problems, but not all steps, are set up.

LEVEL 3

Multiplying and dividing larger and more complicated numbers. Problems are set up in the first three stories.

LEVEL 4

Multiplying and dividing larger and more complicated numbers. Problems are not set up.

ANSWERS

LEVEL 1

Read each story and fill in the blanks as you solve the problems. Problems are set up to guide your work.

Night Owls

Some people do their work at night. I am one of them. I'm a D.J. at WSPR radio. I work from 11:00 p.m. to 6:00 a.m. I talk to my late-night listeners over the air. We call ourselves the Night Owl Club.

Mario Lopez is the night watchman down at the Jacko Company. He calls in requests about twice a week. He makes about _____ requests a month. Good guy, Mario! (1 month = 4 weeks)

(1 month = _____) x _____ = _____ requests a month
           weeks   requests
                      a week

Rosa Jackson is a night nurse at the hospital. She calls in requests for patients. Rosa works 4 nights a week from 11:00 p.m. to 7:00 a.m. She works _____ hours a week. Quiet night, Rosa? Are all the patients doing OK?

_____ x _____ = _____ hours a week
hours a   nights
night   a week

There goes the fire siren! The fire fighters will be at the fire in minutes. There are always people at the station on call. They work 2 days and nights straight. (1 day and night = 24 hours.) Fire fighters here work _____ hours in a shift.

(1 day [day + night] = _____) x _____ = _____ hours in a shift
                  hours   days

Country music is Leroy Morse and Georgie Lee's favorite.
They are ambulance drivers. This month, they are on night
duty. Leroy and Georgie go out on about 5 calls a night.
They work 5 nights a week, so they go on about _____
calls a week.

_____ x _____ = _____ calls a week
calls a   nights
night

Dave Marino is another member of the Night Owl Club.
He drives a taxi three nights a week. He usually drives
about 160 miles in 8 hours. That is an average of
_____ miles in an hour. Are you listening, Davey?
How's business tonight?

_____ ÷ _____ = _____ miles each hour
miles   hours

Officer McKay works night patrol every other week.
He asks me to play cheerful music to keep his spirits up.
The weeks he's on night patrol, he works 7 hours on
5 nights. That comes to _____ hours altogether.
This next song is for you, Officer!

_____ x _____ = _____ hours altogether
hours   nights

Buddy's Café is open all night. Buddy says he likes the
quiet. Last week he worked 54 hours. He was there
6 nights, so he worked _____ hours every night.
Send over a bowl of that good chili, Buddy. Hey, look
at the time! Our night's almost over.

_____ ÷ _____ = _____ hours every night
hours a   nights a
week   week

At the Dime Store

I take care of my five-year-old grandson Jeff on Saturday mornings. Last Saturday it was raining, so we went to the dime store. I gave Jeff a quarter. He headed right for the bubble gum. Kids seem to love gum. I allowed him to buy 3 pieces at 5¢ each. That came to _____¢, so the quarter (was/was not) _____ enough.

$$\underset{\text{pieces}}{\text{_____}} \times \underset{\text{¢ each}}{\text{_____}} = \text{_____¢}$$

Jeff likes to play with those cute little plastic cars. He races them all around the living room. I bought him 4 cars at 20¢ each, which came to _____¢. I put the cars in my bag.

$$\underset{\text{cars}}{\text{_____}} \times \underset{\text{¢ each}}{\text{_____}} = \text{_____¢}$$

We all have a sweet tooth in my family. I enjoy having a chocolate candy after dinner. I bought half a dozen for myself at 5¢ each. I gave the sales clerk a quarter. My quarter (was, was not) _____ enough to pay for the candies. (1 dozen = 12)

$$\underset{\text{candies}}{\text{_____}} \times \underset{\text{¢ each}}{\text{_____}} = \text{_____¢}$$

My memory isn't what it used to be. I have to write notes to myself for everything. If I don't, I forget some of the things I need to do. I was out of note pads, so I bought some new ones. I paid 60¢ for 3 note pads at _____¢ each.

$$\underset{\text{¢ paid}}{\text{_____}} \div \underset{\text{pads}}{\text{_____}} = \text{_____¢ each}$$

By this time, Jeff was running around saying he was hungry. I bought a big package of potato chips with small sacks in it. There are a dozen 2-ounce sacks of potato chips in a package. There are _____ ounces of chips in the whole package.

_____ x _____ = _____ oz., whole package
sacks   oz. (= ounces)
        each sack

I promised Jeff that he could play with the cars and eat some potato chips when we got home. As we were leaving, we passed a sign that said "3 lipsticks for $1." What a buy! I picked up 3 each for myself, my sister, and my friend. Altogether, I bought _____ tubes of lipstick.

_____ x _____ = _____ tubes of lipstick, altogether
lipsticks   people

Jeff was trying to make me hurry up. I had just one more thing to buy. I needed envelopes to send out 24 letters for my husband's business. There are 8 envelopes in a package. I had to buy _____ packages.

_____ ÷ _____ = _____ packages
letters   envelopes
        per package

Keeping Jeff happy and out of trouble is easy at the dime store. At 10:45 a.m., it was time to go. We had been in the store since 9:15 a.m. That was _____ hour and _____ minutes at the dime store. On to the next adventure!

___ : ___ time they left store
– ___ : ___ time they came
————————————————
___ : ___ hour, minutes

Yard Life

I'm Mel Lane, a painter and carpenter. A couple of weeks
ago, I fell off a ladder and broke my leg. Since then,
I've been sitting in my yard watching all the activity.
I'm keeping a journal of what I see. Here are some entries
from it.

Monday:

I watched a honey bee gather nectar. It stopped at 8 flowers
in a 10-minute period. If it keeps that busy, it could visit
_____ flowers in an hour. (1 hour = 60 minutes)

Step one: (1 hour = _____) ÷ 10 minutes = _____ 10-minute periods
　　　　　　　　　　　 minutes

Step two: _____ x _____ = _____ flowers in an hour
　　　　　　 10-min.　　 flowers
　　　　　　 periods　　 in 10 min.

Tuesday:

I watched a praying mantis for a while. It was rather ugly
looking to me. It caught a bug every 6 minutes. In an hour,
it would get _____ bugs. What a lunch!

(1 hour = _____) ÷ _____ = _____ bugs in an hour
　　　　　　 minutes　　 minutes
　　　　　　　　　　　　 per bug

Wednesday:

An old toad sat beside a big rock. An anthill was on
the other side of the rock. Each time an ant came around
the rock, flick! The toad gobbled it up. In 9 minutes, I saw
the toad eat 45 ants. That was _____ ants per minute.

_____ ÷ _____ = _____ ants per minute
ants　　　 minutes

Thursday:

We have a bird house in the yard. I made it for the
purple martins. Each of the 4 sides of the bird house has
5 compartments. Each compartment holds one family
of birds. Altogether, there are _____ compartments

_____ x _____ = _____ compartments
sides   compartments
         per side

Friday:

I have been sitting here for 8 days. In that time, the
sunflower plants have grown 2 feet. That's _____ inches.
What quick growth! They grew _____ inches per day.
(1 foot = 12 inches)

Step one: (1 foot = _____) x _____ = _____ inches in 2 feet
                      inches   feet

Step two: _____ ÷ _____ = _____ inches per day
           inches   days
           in 2 feet

Saturday:

I noticed a spider web covered with dew. The spider was
repairing the web so it could catch some bugs to eat. The
base of the web is about 10 inches long. It is about 8 inches
high, so it covers _____ square inches.

_____ x _____ = _____ square inches
inches   inches
long   high

Sunday:

It rained today, so I'm inside. Tomorrow I get my cast off.
I sure enjoyed sitting outside last week, but I'll be glad
to get back to work.

Before the Knot Is Tied

Julie and Alex got engaged. They decided to wait about
6 months before getting married. That way, they could
save some money first. Julie and Alex had about _____
weeks to wait before their wedding.

(1 month = _____) x _____ = _____ weeks to wait
            weeks   months

Julie worked as a waitress 5 days a week. She decided
to save her tips toward buying some furniture. Her tips
came to about $9 every day. She put $_____ in the bank
every week.

$_____ x _____ = $_____ a week in bank
 tips in   days a
 a day   week

Alex took a weekend job at a garage for extra money.
He worked there 6 hours every weekend. He had the garage
job for 6 weekends. Alex worked _____ hours there.

_____ x _____ = _____ hours worked at garage
hours a   weekends
weekend

When Julie and Alex had saved $150, they bought a sofa.
It was on sale for $230. They put the $150 down and paid
$10 a week. It took _____ weeks to pay the $80 balance.

$_____ ÷ $_____ = _____ weeks to pay balance
 balance   amount
          per week

They also needed bedroom furniture. For $200, they got a headboard, box spring, and mattress. They put down $110, and paid off the $90 balance at $9 a week. It took _____ weeks to finish paying for the bedroom furniture.

$_____ ÷ $_____ = _____ weeks to pay balance
balance   amount per week

At the bridal shower, 3 people each gave matched sets of 6 glasses. Julie and Alex got _____ glasses altogether.

_____ x _____ = _____ glasses altogether
sets   glasses per set

Each of Julie's 8 co-workers at the restaurant gave her a place setting of stainless steel flatware. There were 5 pieces in a set. Julie got _____ pieces of flatware.

_____ x _____ = _____ pieces of flatware
pieces per set   co-workers

Alex's 9 cousins bought the couple a $270 television set. They split the cost equally. They each paid $_____ as their share.

$_____ ÷ _____ = $_____ each
cost of TV   cousins

Julie and Alex were glad they waited. Now they had what they needed to move into their own apartment. They even had enough money saved for a honeymoon.

Fix Up Fairmont!

Fairmont was starting to look run down. The City Council passed some new laws to get the city looking better. Notices were put on the windshields of illegally parked cars. The cars had to be moved within 48 hours. One officer counted 3 dozen illegally parked cars. That was _____ altogether. They had to go!

(1 dozen = _____) x 3 = _____ cars
              cars

Seventeen owners moved their cars. The rest, a total of _____ cars, were towed by the city.

_____ – _____ = _____ cars towed by city
total cars cars moved

Charlie's Towing Service and Gun Hill Garage did all the towing. For 5 days, Charlie's towed 2 cars every day, which came to _____ cars. Gun Hill Garage towed the other 9 cars in 3 days. Gun Hill towed _____ cars per day.

Charlie's: _____ x _____ = _____ cars towed
         days   cars per day

Gun Hill: _____ ÷ _____ = _____ cars per day
       cars   days
       towed

The owners had to claim their cars within 30 days. If they didn't, the cars went to the scrap yard. Only 4 owners came to pay the $50 towing fee. So $_____ was paid for towing.

$_____ x _____ = $_____ paid for towing
towing owners
fee

The scrap yard paid the city $450 for the remaining 15 cars.
The city received $_____ per car.

$_____ ÷ _____ = $_____ per car
  paid by   cars
  scrap yard

One new law said that trucks could not be parked in certain
areas. In one day, police officers ticketed 5 trucks in the city.
They ticketed 3 times that many in other areas. The officers
gave out a total of _____ tickets.

Step one: _____ x _____ = _____ tickets, other areas
       tickets,   times as
       city   many tickets

Step two: _____ + _____ = _____ tickets, total
       tickets,   tickets, city
       other areas

Another new law banned dumping in empty lots. Some lots
were full of garbage and junk. The owner of a lot now had to
pay $2 for removal of every 10 pounds of junk. In one lot,
700 pounds were removed. The owner had to pay $_____.

Step one: _____ ÷ _____ = _____ 10-lb. units
       lbs.   lbs. for $2
       removed

Step two: _____ x $_____ = $_____ paid for removal
    10-lb. units   per 10 lbs.

One corner lot was full of weeds, old tires, and broken
bottles. One day, city workers spent 8 hours cleaning up
the lot. Each worker earned $56. The city paid them
$_____ an hour.

$_____ ÷ _____ = $_____ an hour
  earned   hours

The Magic of Wood

Jane Springer takes shop classes and loves to work with wood. She wants to be a carpenter when she finishes high school next year.

Last spring, Jane made 6 bird houses. She needed a piece of wood for each of the 4 sides, 1 for the bottom, and 2 for the roof. That meant Jane used 7 pieces of wood for each bird house. Altogether, she used _____ pieces of wood.

_____ x _____ = _____ pieces of wood altogether
houses   pieces per house

Jane figured out how to use one board for each bird house. She cut the board into pieces that were each 8 inches long. She needed to get 7 pieces of wood from each board, so the board had to be at least _____ inches long to make one bird house.

_____ x _____ = _____ inch-long board
inches, each piece   pieces

For Christmas, Jane made sets of picture frames for her mother, grandfather, and 2 aunts. There were 4 picture frames in each set. Jane made _____ frames altogether.

_____ x _____ = _____ frames altogether
sets   frames per set

Jane's younger sister collects shells. Jane made her a box with spaces for displaying her collection. There were 6 spaces down and 9 across. One shell went in each space, so the box held _____ shells.

_____ x _____ = _____ spaces for shells, total
spaces   spaces
down   across

Jane and her father made a dog house for Prince, the family dog. For each side, they used 4 boards that were 9 inches wide. The boards were laid one on top of another. The dog house was _____ inches high.

_____ x _____ = _____ inches high
boards   inches
           wide

The dog house was 4 feet long. Each long side took 4 boards. Jane needed _____ feet of lumber for the 2 long sides of the dog house.

(_____ x _____) x _____ = _____ feet of lumber, altogether
boards   feet, long   number of
each side   side   long sides

Jane used 21 ounces of paint for the dog house. She applied 3 coats of paint, using _____ ounces for each coat. Prince's new home looked great. Jane was already a fine carpenter.

_____ ÷ _____ = _____ ounces per coat
ounces   coats
used

LEVEL 2

In this level, you will multiply and divide larger numbers. Problems are set up to guide your work.

Sports Items

Students in the night school math class were always talking about sports. So Mr. Morales, the teacher, asked students to collect information from the sports pages of the local newspaper. They used the information to make up problems.

Gordon Fairway was in the newspaper because he did something very unusual: he got the same score each day of a 4-day golf tournament. His 4-day score was 288, so his score each day was _____.

_____ ÷ _____ = _____ score each day
　score　　　days

The newspaper reported on a race at the auto track. One of the racers, Van Thurman, went 396 miles in 3 hours. His average speed was _____ mph.

_____ ÷ _____ = _____ mph
　miles　　　hours

"Bomber" Janie Smith is the hero of the local high school basketball team. She scored 600 points during the basketball season. She played in 30 games. She scored an average of _____ points per game.

_____ ÷ _____ = _____ points per game
　points　　　games

The basketball team scored 89 points in one game. Nine points were from 1-point free throws. The rest were from 2-point field goals. The team made _____ field goals.

Step one:

_____ points, total

− _____ points, free throws
_____

_____ points, field goals

Step two: _____ ÷ _____ = _____ field goals
points,   points per
field goals field goal

Many area residents have taken up running in the park. The newspaper did a story about local runners. A reporter talked to Edgar Brown. Edgar runs 6 miles every day, which is _____ miles a week.

_____ x _____ = _____ miles a week
miles a   days a
day   week

The newspaper interviewed runners in the annual road race. Anna Dean told a reporter that she trained by running 5 miles every day. She trained every day for 30 days. Anna ran _____ miles to train for the race.

_____ days

x _____ miles a day
_____

_____ miles, training

One of the high school students trained for the race by running 4 miles to school. It took him 24 minutes, 40 seconds. One mile took him _____ minutes and _____ seconds.

_____, _____ ÷ _____ = _____ minutes, _____ seconds per mile
minutes seconds miles

Mr. Morales' students asked to do sports problems more often.

Drivers Talk

Rudy Morris:

My name is Rudy Morris. I've been driving a
bus for the town for eight years. Rain or snow,
I'm out there picking up passengers. My bus
route is 82 miles round-trip. I drive it 3 times
a day. Altogether, I drive _____ miles a day,
always smiling!

_____ miles in route

x _____ times a day

_____

_____ miles a day

The bus is crowded in the morning when people are going
to work. It's emptier in the middle of the day. Altogether,
I take about 96 people on my bus during my 3 daily trips.
That's an average of _____ people per trip.

$$\frac{_____}{\text{people a day}} \div \frac{_____}{\text{trips a day}} = _____ \text{ people per trip}$$

Lindsay Dixon:

Hi, there! I was one of the first woman taxi drivers in town.
It's a great job if you like driving. I meet lots of interesting
people, and I enjoy chatting with them. Most days, I get
about 20 fares and go about 140 miles. That's an average of
_____ miles per fare.

$$\frac{_____}{\text{miles}} \div \frac{_____}{\text{fares}} = _____ \text{ miles per fare}$$

I usually drive to the airport 4 times a day.
Sometimes it's a real rush to get there in time
for a flight. It's 12 miles to the airport and back.
I drive _____ miles just going to and from the
airport every day.

_____ miles, round trip

x _____ times a day

_____

_____ miles a day

Charlie White:

Hi, I'm Charlie. I drive an 18-wheel truck about 420 miles every Monday, Wednesday, and Friday. I deliver goods to companies in nearby towns and cities. By the end of every week, I've driven _____ miles in my truck.

_____ miles a day

x _____ days per week

_____

_____ miles per week

Beebee Jones:

My job is driving a school bus. Nobody messes around on my bus! The kids sure listen to me. There are 33 stops on my route in the morning and the same number in the afternoon. I make these stops every day, Monday to Friday. Every week, I make _____ stops altogether.

Step one: _____ + _____ = _____ stops a day
           stops a.m. stops p.m.

Step two: _____ x _____ = _____ stops a week
          stops a   days a
          day   week

L. J. Stevens:

Want to see a thrilling sight? Come to the auto races this Saturday. I'm driving! Yes, I'm a race-car driver. Last race, I went 101 mph for 9 hours. I drove _____ miles. That was tough!

_____ mph

x _____ hours

_____

_____ miles

One Saturday, I was in a demolition derby. That was great! They paid me $800 for every 30-minute period that the car was still running. I kept going for an hour and a half, or 3 periods. I earned $_____. I really earned it!

$ _____ per period

x _____ periods

_____

$ _____ earnings

20

Thursday Grocery Shopping

On sale! Bananas: 37¢ per lb.

When I get home from work on Thursdays, I read the grocery store ads in the newspaper. Then I check my shopping list and gather my coupons. The evening is a good, quiet time to shop.

I started in the produce section tonight. I picked up potatoes, onions, lettuce, broccoli, and cabbage. Then I got some fruit. I bought 2 pounds of bananas, which cost me _____¢.

_____¢ per lb.

x _____ lbs.
_____

_____¢ for bananas

Apples: 3 lbs. for 99¢

My son Pete and I live alone, so I don't buy too much at once. Pete likes to take an apple in his lunch. I bought five apples, which weighed 2 pounds. I paid _____¢ for them.

Step one: _____¢ ÷ _____ = _____¢ per lb.
          per 3 lbs.   lbs. for 99¢

Step two:

_____¢ per lb.

x _____ lbs.
_____

_____¢ for 2 lbs.

Extra special! Tuna fish: 5 cans for $3.55

The tuna fish was a really good deal. We eat a lot of it. We both like tuna salad, and tuna noodle casserole is one of our favorites. The cans cost only _____¢ each on sale.

$_____ ÷ _____ = _____¢ per can
  cost,   cans
  5 cans

Rolls: 20¢ each! Regularly 25¢

There are different types of rolls: rye, pumpernickel, onion, and poppyseed. I bought a dozen rolls, three of each kind. The total cost was $_____.

_____ x _____¢ = _____¢ = $_____ cost, rolls
rolls   each

On sale! Peanut cookies: $2.00 per box

After I got milk, eggs, and cheese, I went to the cookie section. I love to have a cookie or two after dinner. The cookies I like are usually $2.29 a box. Today they were on sale and I had a 50¢ coupon. I picked up 2 boxes. That means I saved _____¢ on peanut cookies.

Well, that was a great shopping trip. Almost everything I needed was on sale.

Step one:

$ _____ regular price, 1 box

x _____ boxes
_____

$ _____ regular price, 2 boxes

Step two:

$ _____ regular price, 2 boxes

– _____ sale price, 2 boxes
_____

$ _____ savings, 2 boxes

Step three:

_____¢ savings, 2 boxes

+ _____¢ coupon
_____

_____¢ = $_____ total saved

Kokomo Recycling Center

Things we used to call garbage can often
be used again.

The Kokomo Recycling Center (KRC) gets
4 deliveries of material from smaller recycling
centers every month. Each delivery includes
205 tons of newspaper, glass, aluminum cans,
and other materials. That comes to _____
tons of material a month.

_____ tons per delivery

x _____ deliveries a month

_____ tons of material a month

- -

Paper is made from trees. It can also be made
from recycled paper. Recycling paper saves
trees. One load of old newspaper from KRC
saves 70 trees. KRC sends 8 loads each month
to paper mills. Recycling those 8 loads saves
_____ trees per month.

_____ trees saved, one load

x _____ loads per month

_____ trees saved per month

- -

The National Aluminum Company collects
empty soda cans 3 times a month. The company
could use all new aluminum to make new cans.
That would cost $45,000 per month. If they
use recycled aluminum from KRC, it only costs
$4,500 per month. That is a savings of
$_____ per collection.

Step one:

$ _____ cost of new aluminum

− _____ cost of recycled cans

$ _____ savings per month

Step two: $_____ ÷ _____ = $_____ savings per collection
         savings   collections
         per month per month

23

Fifty-six organizations have accounts with KRC. Girl Scout Troop 468 is one of them. The girl scouts collect used glass to raise funds. This week, they came in with 3 boxes of glass. Each box weighed 40 pounds. KRC pays 3¢ a pound for glass. So this week, Girl Scout Troop 468 was credited $_____.

Step one:

_____ lbs. each box of glass

x _____ boxes of glass

_____

_____ lbs. of glass

Step two:

_____ lbs. of glass

x _____ ¢ per lb.

_____

_____ ¢ = $_____ credited

- -

Some churches collect newspapers to raise money. Last month, one church group came with a whole truckload. The newspapers weighed 738 pounds. KRC pays 2¢ per pound for newspapers. The church's account was credited $_____.

_____ pounds

x _____ ¢ per pounds

_____

_____ ¢ = $_____ credited

KRC isn't the only kind of recycling center. Getting rid of old tires can be a problem. But they can be recycled, too. Some energy plants burn tires to get power. One tire is equal to 2 gallons of oil in such a plant. A local plant once burned 640 gallons of oil per day. Now it burns _____ tires to get the same power. Talk about "burning rubber"!

_____ ÷ _____ = _____ tires burned per day
gallons   gallons
of oil   per tire

LEVEL 3

In this level, you will multiply and divide larger and more complicated numbers. Some problems are not set up.

Installments

Most people don't pay for large purchases all at once. Instead, they pay in installments over a period of months or years. Stella Gold and her husband Wayne use installments to help buy what they need. It works for them because they always make their payments on time.

Stella:

When we first married, we just had Wayne's old TV. When it broke, we bought a new TV on sale for $180. Our down payment was $30. We paid the balance off in 6 monthly payments. Each payment was $_____.

Step one: $_____ − $_____ = $_____ amount to pay
            cost   down payment

Step two: $_____ ÷ _____ = $_____ a month
           amount   payments
           to pay

We sold our old sofa and chairs to a used furniture store for $40. We used that $40 as a down payment on a new maple sofa and chair set that cost $640. We paid the balance off in one year at $_____ a month.

Step one: $_____ − $_____ = $_____ amount to pay
            cost   down payment

Step two: $_____ ÷ _____ = $_____ a month
           amount   payments
           to pay

Soon we had our first child. The medical bills were high.
The insurance covered the hospital bill and half the
doctor's fee. We paid the doctor $612 altogether, in
9 monthly payments. We paid $_____ a month.
Wayne, Jr., was worth it!

$_____ ÷ _____ = $_____ per month
  amount   payments
  to pay

We decided to buy a bigger car. We got $200 for our old car.
We used that $200 as a down payment on a car that cost
$3,800. We paid the balance, $_____, in a year and a half.
The monthly payments were $_____.

Step one: $_____ − $_____ = $_____ amount to pay
           cost of   down
           new car   payment

Step two: $_____ ÷ _____ = $_____ a month
           amount   months
           to pay

We don't use our charge card too often. We did use it to pay
our motel bill on a recent trip. We spent 4 nights in the
motel, and the bill was $268. That was $_____ per night.

$_____ ÷ _____ = $_____ per night
  bill   nights

When we had saved enough money, we bought a house.
We pay the mortgage once a month. It's $390 a month.
Our mortgage payments total $_____ a year. These have
been our biggest installment payments ever!

$_____ x _____ = $_____ a year
  monthly   months
  payment

Buttery Bakery

What's good about the bakery where I work?
We sell the most delicious treats in town. What's
bad about the bakery? We sell the most calories.

George and Marco start baking at 5:00 a.m.
Marco makes 4 large sheet cakes every day:
chocolate, spice, coconut, and lemon. He cuts
each cake into 48 pieces. We have _____
pieces of cake to sell.

_____ pieces per cake

x _____ cakes

_____

_____ pieces to sell

- -

Marco also bakes 9 kinds of cookies daily. My
favorites are the chocolate chip, pecan crunch,
and oatmeal cookies. He makes 10 dozen of each
kind. That's _____ cookies every day.

_____ each kind (one dozen x 10)

x _____ kinds

_____

_____ cookies every day

George makes the bread and rolls. He makes a total of
12 dozen rolls a day. He makes equal numbers of
pumpernickel rolls, rye rolls, and hard rolls. He makes
_____ of each kind of roll.

(one dozen x 12) $\underset{\text{rolls, total}}{_____}$ ÷ $\underset{\text{kinds}}{_____}$ = _____ each kind of roll

Ms. Erhard, the owner of the bakery, loves to make donuts.
She makes 240 donuts every Saturday. She makes the
same number of plain, sugared, cinnamon, and chocolate-
covered donuts. She makes _____ of each kind of donut.
They're all delicious!

$\underset{\text{donuts}}{_____}$ ÷ $\underset{\text{kinds}}{_____}$ = _____ each kind of donut

Hal Jones comes in every other day to get some bread and to talk to George. George's rye bread is Hal's favorite. Yesterday, Hal bought a loaf of rye bread at 98¢, and 6 rolls at 20¢ each. I rang up his purchase of $_____.

(_____¢ x _____) + _____¢ = _____ total bill
  each   rolls   bread

On Mondays, Wednesdays, and Fridays, George makes coffee cakes: apple, cinnamon and raisin, cheese, and pecan. Mrs. Morgan gets one kind every week. The cakes cost $4.75 each, so she spends $_____ a month on coffee cakes.

$_____ x _____ = $_____ spent on cakes per month
 each   weeks per
        month

Marco makes pies every Wednesday, Saturday, and Sunday. Most of the pies are made to order. Last week, he made 5 pies to order on Wednesday, 7 on Saturday, and 8 on Sunday. The pies cost $4.50 each, so we took in $_____ for pies ordered last week.

Step one: _____ + _____ + _____ = _____ pies ordered
        Wed.   Sat.   Sun.

Step two: $_____ x _____ = $_____ total
       each   pies ordered

Ms. Steele bought 2 pies at $4.50 each, 2 loaves of bread at 98¢ each, and a cake for $4.75. She gave me a $20 bill and I gave her $_____ in change.

Step one: ($_____ x 2) + ($_____ x 2) + $_____ = $_____ total
     per pie   bread   cake

Step two: $_____ – $_____ = $_____ in change
     bill   total cost

"Look in the Papers"

I graduated from high school in June. I'm not sure what kind of work I want to do. "Look in the papers," everyone told me. Here are some of the jobs I saw offered.

Turn-back agent for Drive-Right Car Rental. 18 yrs. old. Driver's license. $4.75/hr.
This one's for a turn-back agent. I seem to fit the bill. I wonder if I'd have to wash and clean the cars? I'll call to find out more details. I could make $_____ in an 8-hour day.

$ _____ an hour

x _____ hours

_____

$ _____ a day

- -

Decorating firm needs plasterers. $10–$15 hr., depends on experience. Will train.
Now this could lead somewhere. I liked working on a construction site last summer. A plasterer makes good money. In a few months I could be making $12 an hour. That would be $_____ in a 40-hour week.

$ _____ an hour

x _____ hours

_____

$ _____ a week

Truck driver for small firm. $260 per 40-hour week. Driver's license.
I'd like to drive a truck. I wonder what I'd be delivering? I wonder how far I'd have to drive? The pay is better than some of the other jobs. I could make $_____ an hour.

$_____ ÷ _____ = $_____ an hour
per week   hours
        per week

Pest control technician. Will train.
$1,125 per month + benefits.

Hmmm, what about this one? That's a pretty good salary. I need benefits, too. I don't think I'd like working with all those chemicals every day, though. I won't apply, even though I'd earn $_____ a week.

$\underset{\text{a month}}{_____} \div \underset{\text{weeks}}{_____} = \$_____ \text{ a week}$

Accountant's assistant for ad agency.
$1,320/month to start.

Well, I can forget this one. I don't like the idea of sitting still all day. I'd rather do something where I was moving around more. The money's good, though. In that position I could make $_____ a week, just to start.

$\underset{\text{a month}}{_____} \div \underset{\text{weeks}}{_____} = \$_____ \text{ a week}$

Nurse's aides and R.N.s needed.
Aides: $9.25 per hour. Nights, weekends.
R.N.s: $24.25 per hour. Set own time.

Maybe I should think about going to nursing school. I'll have to get some information about nursing programs. I'd really like to be a nurse. It's an important job, and there's usually plenty of work. A nurse's aide earns $_____ in an 8-hour shift. A registered nurse can earn $_____ in 8 hours.

Yes, I think that's what I'll aim for. So I only need to look in the paper for a temporary job.

$ _____ $ an hour (aide)

x _____ hours

_____

$ _____ $ in 8 hours (aide)

- -

$ _____ $ an hour (R.N.)

x _____ hours

_____

$ _____ $ in 8 hours (R.N.)

Photographer

My hobby is photography. Give me any kind of scene and I'm clicking away. On my last vacation I used 4 rolls of film. There were 24 pictures on each roll of film. I shot a total of _____ pictures.

I used up my film at 3 different sites: by the lake, on the mountain top, and at our campground. There were some great shots. I took the same number of pictures at each site. I took _____ pictures at each place.

I work at Brown's Photo Shop 8 hours a week. That helps pay for my hobby and I learn about photography. The manager shows me how to develop and enlarge pictures. He lets me use the darkroom at no charge. I earn $5.50 an hour, which adds up to $_____ a week.

I spend the money I earn at Brown's on photography supplies. Last week, I bought 3 quarts of developing solution at $4.75 a quart and 2 rolls of color film at $7.25 a roll. I also bought a new developing tray for $3.50. After buying these supplies, I had $_____ left in my paycheck.

Although photography is my hobby, sometimes I sell my pictures. At the County Fair, I ran a photography booth. I took pictures of people. I also photographed Mary Taylor's cat and Joe Maron's dog. I took 85 pictures each day. I was there on Friday, Saturday, and Sunday. Altogether, I took _____ pictures.

I photographed my cousin's wedding in June. I shot 1 roll of film at the bride's home, and 2 rolls at the church. Then I shot 4 rolls at the reception and 1 roll as the bride and groom were leaving for their honeymoon. With 36 pictures on each roll, I took _____ pictures of the wedding. That should be enough for any couple.

My cousin paid my expenses. The film for the wedding cost $64. Each roll cost $_____.

I enlarged some of my cousin's wedding pictures. I sold 7 of them to the family for $9.95 each. I got $_____ from selling the enlargements.

I wanted to take some black-and-white pictures at the winter snow carnival. I bought black-and-white film at $3.98 a roll. I bought 4 rolls of film and spent $_____.

People take videos of everything these days. I took videos at the senior prom and at the high school graduation. I edited the videos, made copies, and sold 37 of them at $30 each. My expenses were $68, so I made $_____.

Some day, I'd like to turn my hobby into a full-time job. For now I'm happy working at the photo shop and taking pictures on the side.

Corn Festival

The sign at the Maywood Corn Festival says, "If you don't like corn, stay home!" The Corn Festival raises money for the local health clinic. Last year, 9,060 people attended the festival each night. Friday, Saturday, and Sunday, a total of _____ people attended the Corn Festival.

Each person paid $2.50 to get into the festival. The money from entrance fees came to a total of $_____.

Cowboys and cowgirls on horseback directed traffic and helped park cars. Six pastures were used as parking lots. Each parking lot held about 850 cars. About _____ cars could park at the Corn Festival.

There were tractor pulls and horse-pulling contests. A team of oxen even tried for a prize. The horse-pulling contests were the most exciting. The winning team of 2 horses pulled 1,750 pounds. Each horse pulled _____ pounds.

Corn patch dolls are very popular at the festival.
Mrs. Morley ran the doll booth last year. She hired 7 people to make 80 dolls each. She had _____ corn patch dolls to sell in the booth. Every single doll was sold by the end of the festival.

Other booths sell items made from corn husks, kernels of corn, and corncobs. These booths had sales of $2,520 last year. This money is always divided into 3 equal parts.
One part goes to pay expenses, one part goes to the people running the booths, and one part goes to the clinic.
The clinic got $_____ last year.

At the stadium nearby, there is a concert each night of the festival. There are 4 entry gates to the stadium. At last year's country music concert, 2,450 people entered at each gate. A total of _____ people went to hear the music.

Everyone loves the contests for the best large animals, poultry, and vegetables raised or grown on corn farms. An equal number of first, second, and third prizes are given in each contest. There were 168 prizes awarded last year. _____ of those were first prizes.

People come from miles around to eat the corn dinners. A record 63,376 ears of corn were cooked and served last year. Each dinner included 4 ears of corn. A total of _____ corn dinners were sold at last year's festival.

The regular corn dinners cost $4.25 each. There was corn relish, corn salad, corn pone, corn fritters, corn puddings, and even corn ice cream. The caterers took in $35,984.75 from regular dinners. They served _____ regular dinners.

The jumbo dinners always include ham or barbecue and all the corn you can eat. The caterers served 3,456 jumbo dinners at $8 each. Festival goers spent $_____ on jumbo dinners last year.

The first Maywood Corn Festival was held in 1906. It's been held every year since then. So far, there have been _____ Corn Festivals in Maywood.

LEVEL 4

In this level, you will have to set up all your own problems on the right side of the page.

The Patio

Last summer, Mr. Wharton and his son Russ built a brick patio in their backyard. First, they measured the available space. Then, they drew a plan for the patio. They decided to make it 20 feet long and 12 feet wide. That's _____ square feet.

Bricks are measured in inches, not feet. Mr. Wharton asked Russ to figure out how long and wide the patio would be in inches. Russ told his dad that the length, 20 feet, is _____ inches. The width of the patio, 12 feet, is _____ inches.

The bricks Mr. Wharton wanted to use were 8 inches long and 4 inches wide. He planned to lay the bricks end to end on the long side of the patio. He would need _____ bricks to total 20 feet.

Russ laid the bricks side by side on the short side of the patio. He needed _____ bricks to fill in a 12-foot row.

Mr. Wharton asked Russ to figure out the exact number of bricks needed to complete the patio. Russ counted the number of bricks on each side. He multiplied the two numbers to find the exact number of bricks in the patio. They needed exactly _____ bricks.

Mr. Wharton knew of an old brick building that was being torn down. The owner charged $1 for every dozen bricks, no matter what condition. Mr. Wharton needed 1,452 bricks to be sure to get enough good ones. That would cost $_____.

To compare, Mr. Wharton also got a cost estimate for new bricks. New bricks would cost 30¢ each. Mr. Wharton would save $_____ by buying old bricks.

Mr. Wharton liked the old bricks better anyway once he and Russ cleaned them up. They cleaned bricks from 6:00 p.m. to 8:00 p.m. every evening from Monday to Friday. Between them, they spent a total of _____ hours cleaning bricks.

One weekend, they measured and marked the 12-foot by 20-foot area that they had chosen for the patio. They dug down eight inches to level the area. They needed a metal edging to support the sides of the patio. The edging went all the way around. It was _____ feet long.

Before they put the bricks down, they inserted a plastic lining. The lining had to cover the whole 12-foot by 20-foot area. Mr. Wharton paid 60¢ a square foot for the lining. The cost for the plastic lining was $_____.

Finally, they laid down the bricks and sprinkled the patio with sand. Once it was swept and watered, it looked great! Since Mr. Wharton and Russ did the work themselves, the patio didn't cost too much, either.

Leaving Home

It's been a couple of years since I finished high school. I'm still getting used to taking care of myself. It's taken a while to get used to doing that.

In high school, I had a weekend job at Farley's Garage. When I got out of school, I knew I wanted to be a mechanic. Mr. Farley said he would give me a job as a regular mechanic. He said I should take a course in mechanics first. My father loaned me $240 to pay for the course. I paid him back $10 a week. I paid the money back in _____ weeks. That's about _____ months.

When I finished the course, Mr. Farley kept his promise. He hired me as a regular mechanic. Even after taking the course, I still have a lot to learn. I work 40 hours a week at $8 an hour. Mr. Farley pays me $_____ every Friday.

I soon learned that I don't take home all the money I earn. I have to pay Social Security, health insurance, and income tax. I only take home $256. My mother advised me to save $75 a week for a car. I figured if I saved $75 a week for 6 months, I would have $_____ to buy a car.

After six months, I bought a used car. I also decided to move away from home. My friends Luis and Steve and I looked for an apartment. We looked at several and found one we liked. It would cost us $150 each for rent per month, plus utilities. We split the utilities 3 ways. The first month's gas bill was $36, the electric bill was $69, and the phone bill was $34.50. That first month, we each paid $_____ in rent and utilities.

The three of us share the shopping and cooking. I buy the main groceries once a week. I usually spend around $50. Luis buys fruit and vegetables a couple of times a week for about $25 a week. Steve spends around $30 a week on soda, cleaning and paper products, and any extra things we need. At the end of each week, we divide the costs evenly. We each pay about $_____ a week.

My trip to work is longer now that I've moved. I used to drive 3 miles to get to work. Now I drive 7 miles twice a day, 5 days a week, 4 weeks a month. That adds up to _____ extra miles a month.

Now that I'm away from home, my expenses have all gone up. To earn some spending money I have a part-time job on Friday and Saturday nights. I'm a waiter at the steak house on Route 10, just past the mall. I don't get paid much, but the tips are great. I usually make $75 in an evening. That's an extra $_____ per month.

With all this work, I'm ready for a vacation. Luis, Steve, and I want to go camping and hiking in the Great Smoky Mountains in June. That's 5 months from now. We'll have to pay for transportation, a tent, sleeping bags, backpacks, and food. We figure the trip will cost us each $450. I need to save $_____ a week between now and June.

By then, it'll be three years since I was in high school. I guess you could say I'm really an adult now.

The Implosion

October:

Boom! Boom! The abandoned warehouse that had covered a whole square block fell inward. The newspapers called it an "implosion."

Ardella Brooks and Carlie Hernández were thrilled. The warehouse had attracted vandals to their neighborhood. Since April 1, the women had each spent about 3 hours a week planning a protest. They wanted the city to tear down the building. The city finally tore the building down on October 31. Ardella and Carlie had each spent about _____ hours planning the protest.

November:

Bulldozers cleared the lot where the warehouse had been. Truckloads of material were taken away. Most of the lot was smoothed over. Workers and machines woke up the neighborhood at 7:00 a.m. They worked for 9 hours a day, until _____ p.m. Noise! Noise! Noise!

December:

The city finished cleaning up the lot. There were still problems, however. Children were getting hurt on pieces of glass and metal every day. The lot needed a fence. The lot was 345 feet long and 150 feet wide. To enclose the lot, _____ feet of fence were needed.

January:

Snow fell and the children weren't playing outside much. The city put off building the fence. At $10 a foot, the fence would cost $_____. That was money the city did not have. A fence post had to go up every 10 feet. To reach all the way around the lot, _____ posts were needed.

February:

Nothing had been done, so Ardella and Carlie held a meeting. Everyone agreed that the lot could be improved. "I always wanted to grow my own tomatoes," someone said. An idea was born! The lot was 345 feet by 150 feet, which was _____ square feet. That was good space for growing things!

March:

Sixty-two families in the neighborhood said they would like to have a garden. The lot still had to be fenced. The city agreed to buy the fencing if the residents would put it up. Fourteen residents offered to spend 4 hours each putting up the fence. So, _____ hours of labor were available.

April:

The city parks department donated 12 truckloads of soil and peat moss. Each of the 62 families would have 600 square feet to grow whatever they wanted. Family gardens would take up _____ square feet of lot.

The rest of the lot would be made into a playground. The playground would be _____ square feet.

May:

The parks department donated some trees and bushes. There was room for paths, grass, and some benches. Thirty-four residents agreed to help maintain the area. It took 136 hours a month, on average, to keep it in good shape. Each resident spent _____ hours per month. It was an "implosion" of green!

Bill's Hot Dogs

Bill saved enough money to start his own business.
He bought a used hot dog stand for $750. He put $150
down. He has to pay off the rest in 6 months. He sets aside
$_____ each week for the payment.

Bill uses his car to tow the stand to different spots.
He spends $32 per month on gas to move the stand.
He also has to buy butane gas for the grill. This costs
$60 a month. He figures his expenses weekly. He budgets
$_____ per week for both kinds of gas.

Insurance is one of Bill's big expenses. He pays $264 every
3 months for insurance on the stand and his car. If he lost
the stand, Bill would lose his business. He needs good
insurance. He budgets $_____ per week for insurance.

Hot dogs and hot dog buns don't stay fresh for long. Bill
buys supplies at least once a week. This week, Bill bought
75 pounds of hot dogs for $1.20 a pound. He also bought
60 dozen hot dog buns at 8 for 30¢. He spent $_____
on hot dogs and buns this week.

Bill had to get other supplies this week, too. He bought
37 cases of soda at $5 a case, 2 gallons of mustard
at $1 a quart, and 2 gallons of relish at $2 a quart.
Altogether, Bill paid $_____ for these other supplies.
(1 gallon = 4 quarts)

Customers don't just want hot dogs. They often get snacks, like chips, as well. This week, Bill bought 1,200 bags of snacks at 50 for $7.50. The snacks cost him $_____.

Bill sold 900 cans of soda at 75¢ each, and 1,200 bags of snacks at 40¢ each. He took in $_____ on soda and snacks this week.

Bill likes to know how much he earns by selling soda and snacks. To do this, Bill subtracts the amount he pays for soda and snacks (expenses) from the amount he gets from selling them (gross income). This is his net income on soda and snacks. (Gross income minus expenses = net income.) Bill's net income on soda and snacks was $_____.

Some weeks, Bill does good business. Other weeks, it's not so good. It depends on the weather and where he parks the stand. Bill parked his stand in some busy areas this week. Business was pretty good. He sold 600 hot dogs at $1.10 each. His gross income was $_____ on hot dogs.

At the end of each week, Bill figures out his gross income. That is the total amount of money he takes for everything he sells. This week he took in $_____. Then he figures out his net income. That is the total amount he took minus the total cost of running his stand. His total costs include payment for the stand, insurance, gas, and all the food and soda supplies. This week, Bill's net income was $_____.

Bill keeps track of all his expenses. He saves as much as he can. One day, Bill hopes to sell the hot dog stand and buy his own restaurant.

South Philly

I am Enrico Marino. My friends call me "Rico." My family lives in South Philadelphia. My mother shops at the outdoor market there every Saturday morning.

Today she got 8 huge oranges at 4 for $1, 2 pineapples at 69¢ each, 2 pounds of grapes at 77¢ a pound, and 2 melons at 49¢ each. She got _____¢ in change from $6.

She went to the vegetable stand next. She bought three bunches of broccoli for a total of 99¢, three pounds of carrots for $1, 3 pounds of potatoes at 39¢ a pound, 2 pounds of onions at 29¢ a pound, and 3 large eggplants at 45¢ each. The total cost of the vegetables was $_____.

Mom always stops at the cheese stand. Today she bought 3 pounds of ricotta cheese at $1.49 a pound. She picked out 2 small balls of mozzarella cheese at $1.35 each. She also got an 8-ounce piece of cheddar cheese at $3.30 a pound. She spent $_____ on cheese this Saturday.
(16 ounces = 1 pound)

Mom shops at different meat stands. She got a 6-pound rack of lamb at $1.89 a pound at Tony's Lamb Stand. She picked up 5 pounds of spare ribs at $1.39 a pound at the pork truck. At Booker's Beef, she got 4 pounds of lean ground beef at $1.29 a pound. The cost of meat this week was $_____.

I usually go to buy the pasta and the bread. Today, I got 2 pounds of ziti macaroni at 59¢ a pound. I bought 3 crusty, warm loaves of bread for 89¢ each. For a treat, I got 5 Italian pastries, one for each of member of the family. They cost 79¢ each. My change from a $10 bill was $_____.

I always have spending money when I go to the market. After school, I earn money by cleaning my uncle's shop. He says I can join the business when I'm older. I work different hours there every week. Last week, I worked for 7 hours at $3.69 an hour. My pay last week was $_____.

My friend Nick sells shopping bags to tourists. They can't resist the deals at the market. Nick buys 100 bags for $15. He makes a good profit. He sells the bags for 35¢ each, so his profit on 100 bags is $_____.

When Nick is done working on Saturdays, we visit the stands. We never miss a bargain. Today, we each bought a t-shirt for $7.98 apiece. Nick got a cap for $3.49. Altogether, we paid $_____ for our clothes.

After we'd visited some stands, we both had a Philly steak-and-cheese sandwich for lunch. I paid for lunch this week. Each sandwich was $2.20, and our drinks were 35¢ each. I had only $5 left, so Nick lent me a _____ (coin).

Shopping at the outdoor market is a lot of fun. I spend about $12 there every Saturday. In a year, I spend $_____ at the outdoor market. (1 year = 52 weeks)

Westward, Ho!

1803:

President Jefferson started the Lewis and Clark Expedition. It explored the Louisiana Territory and the Oregon Territory. The expedition began in September, 1803, and reached the Pacific Ocean in November, 1805. The journey covered 2,500 miles and took 26 months. It went an average of _____ miles a month. (Round off to the nearest mile.)

1825:

Pioneers traveled west on the Erie Canal from the Hudson River to Lake Erie, a trip of 363 miles. The Canal cost $7,143,789 when it was finished in 1825. It cost $_____ per mile. (Round off to the nearest dollar.)

Seventy-foot-long boats traveled on the Erie Canal. Horses walking beside the canal pulled the boats. People paid for their trips by the mile. The average price was 25¢ a mile. The total cost for the 363-mile trip was $_____.

1840:

Many people went west on the Oregon Trail in the 1840s. The journey from Iowa to Oregon is about 1,600 miles. The average speed was 12 miles a day, so it took about _____ days to get there. (Round off to the nearest day.)

1870:

It is 300 miles from New Orleans to St. Louis on the Mississippi River. Riverboat races used to be held along that route. It took the boats 3 days and 20 hours to travel that distance. (1 day = 24 hours.) At that rate, they traveled _____ miles per hour. (Round off to the nearest mile.)

ANSWERS: Self-Check

LEVEL 1

Night Owls (p. 5)
8 requests a month

32 hours a week

48 hours in a shift

25 calls a week

20 miles each hour

35 hours altogether

9 hours every night

At the Dime Store (p. 7)
15¢ for gum;
quarter *was* enough

80¢ for cars

30¢ for candies;
quarter *was not* enough

20¢ each

24 ounces of chips

9 tubes of lipstick

3 packages of envelopes

1 hour and 30 minutes at store

Yard Life (p. 9)
6 periods; 48 flowers in hour

10 bugs in an hour

5 ants per minute

20 compartments

24 inches; 3 inches per day

80 square inches

Before the Knot Is Tied (p. 11)
24 weeks to wait

$45 a week in bank

36 hours worked at garage

8 weeks, sofa

10 weeks, bedroom

18 glasses altogether

40 pieces of flatware

$30 each for television

Fix Up Fairmont! (p. 13)
36 cars

19 towed by city

10 cars, Charlie's;
3 cars per day, Gun Hill

$200 paid for towing

$30 per car

15 tickets; 20, total

70 units; $140 paid for removal

$7 an hour

The Magic of Wood (p. 15)
42 pieces of wood

56 inches long

16 frames

54 spaces for shells

36 inches high

32 feet of lumber

7 ounces each coat

LEVEL 2

Sports Items (p. 17)
72 each day

132 mph

20 points per game

80 points; 40 field goals

42 miles a week

150 miles training

6 minutes, 10 seconds per mile

Drivers Talk (p. 19)
246 miles a day

32 people per trip

7 miles per fare

48 miles a day

1,260 miles per week

66 stops a day;
  330 stops a week

909 miles

$2,400 earnings

Thursday Grocery Shopping (p. 21)
74¢ for bananas

33¢ per pound;
  66¢ for two pounds

71¢ per can

$2.40, cost of rolls

$4.58 regular price;
  58¢ savings;
  $1.08, total saved

Kokomo Recycling Center (p. 23)
820 tons

560 trees

$40,500 per month;
  $13,500 per collection

120 pounds;
  $3.60 credited

$14.76 credited to church

320 tires

LEVEL 3

Installments (p. 25)
$150 to pay on TV;
  $25 a month

$600 to pay on furniture;
  $50 a month

$68 a month, doctor's bill

$3600 to pay on car;
  $200 a month

$67 per night

$4,680 a year

Buttery Bakery (p. 27)
192 pieces

1,080 cookies

48 of each kind of roll

60 of each kind of donut

$2.18, Hal's bill

$19 a month

20 pies ordered;
  $90 for pies

$15.71 total;
  $4.29 in change

"Look in the Papers" (p. 29)
$38 in eight-hour day

$480 in 40-hour week

$6.50 an hour

$281.25 a week, pest control

$330 a week, ad agency

$74, nurse's aide;
  $194, R.N.

Photographer (p. 31)
96 pictures

32 pictures at each place

$44 a week

$11.75 left

255 pictures at fair

288 pictures of wedding

$8 each roll

$69.65 from enlargements

$15.92 for film

$1,042 made on videos

Corn Festival (p. 33)
27,180 people

$67,950 in entrance fees

5,100 cars

875 pounds each

560 corn patch dolls

$840 for clinic

9,800 people

56 first prizes

15,844 corn dinners

8,467 regular dinners

$27,648 on jumbo dinners

Answers will vary.

LEVEL 4

The Patio (p. 35)

240 square feet

240 inches long;
144 inches wide

30 bricks to total 20 feet

36 bricks for 12-foot row

1,080 bricks needed

$121 for old bricks

$324 for new bricks;
$203 saved

20 hours

64 feet long

$144 for plastic lining

Leaving Home (p. 37)

24 weeks; 6 months

$320 every Friday

$1,800 for car

$196.50 each, first month

$35 each a week

160 extra miles

$600 extra

$22.50 a week

The Implosion (p. 39)

84 hours each

4:00 p.m.

990 feet of fence

$9,900 for fence;
99 posts needed

51,750 square feet

56 hours of labor

37,200 square feet, gardens;
14,550 square feet, playground

4 hours each

Bill's Hot Dogs (p. 41)

$25 per week, payment

$23 per week, gas

$22 per week, insurance

$117 for hot dogs and buns

$209 for other supplies

$180 for snacks

$1,155 on soda and snacks

$790, net income, soda and snacks

$660, gross income, hot dogs

$1,815, gross income altogether;
$1,239, net income altogether

South Philly (p. 43)

10¢ change

$5.09 for vegetables

$8.82 for cheese

$23.45, cost of meat

$2.20 change

$25.83, pay last week

$20 profit

$19.45 for clothes

10¢; a *dime*

$624 in a year

Westward, Ho! (p. 45)

96 miles a month

$19,680 per mile

$90.75 for trip

133 days

3 miles per hour